glimmers
*

glim

A
Practice
for
Capturing
Daily
Moments
of
Joy

mers

CHRONICLE BOOKS

SAN FRANCISCO

ISBN 978-1-7972-3404-5

Manufactured in China.

MIX
Paper | Supporting
responsible forestry
FSC™ C008047

Design by Vanessa Dina.
Text by Alexandra Galou.

10 9 8 7 6 5 4 3 2 1

Chronicle books and gifts are available at special
quantity discounts to corporations, professional
associations, literacy programs, and other orga-
nizations. For details and discount information,
please contact our premiums department at
corporatesales@chroniclebooks.com or at
1-800-759-0190.

Chronicle Books LLC
680 Second Street
San Francisco, California 94107
www.chroniclebooks.com

introduction

Welcome to a new kind of gratitude journaling practice. Instead of recording big moments few and far between to feel thankful for, use *Glimmers* to seek out and mark small moments of joy—moments that frequently get overlooked when recalling the day's events.

Often described as the opposite of emotional triggers, glimmers are micro moments that usher in feelings of joy, calm, or an appreciation for life. When experiencing a glimmer, even for a brief moment, all is right in the world, the body and mind are content, and a smile slowly buds from deep within.

A glimmer can be a fleeting delight that leaves you feeling full: your favorite song playing in the grocery store, a coffee made with the perfect amount of milk, a podcast release you've been waiting all week for that makes focus hours fly by, catching the train right on time, or the feeling of a clean, warm, fluffy towel fresh from the laundry after a long day of work.

Our gratitude is often reserved for momentous occasions or unspecific areas of life, such as work, family, upcoming vacations, and

material possessions. How often do we get to relish the small, quiet, and intimate moments that comprise the bulk of our lives? Sometimes the smile from a stranger on your way to work is the one thing keeping you together for the day—that, just as much as anything, deserves a nod of recognition.

So, allow this journal to be a dedicated place to store and record glimmers. Here's to focusing on the little, shining moments that give life a bit of sparkle between the big occasions!

how
to
use
this
journal

This journal follows a two-step process for cultivating a glimmer mindset: setting intentions and recording. To reap the full benefits of glimmers, it's crucial to remember that they're easy to brush over if approached without intention—the more one sets to seek out glimmers, the more often they will appear. Equally important, writing your glimmers down will help train your brain to recognize them.

The first step is to set a **daily glimmer intention.**

Ask yourself this: Where and when will I look for glimmers? At what moments of my day will I stop, take a breath, and assess my surroundings? How many glimmers will I try to seek out before I leave work? Is there someone whom I would like to share a glimmer with?

The second step encourages **recording your findings.**

Where did you notice moments of contentment? What about them brought you joy? Was it an unexpected glimmer, or had you anticipated it?

example

Where and when will I look for glimmers today?

1. At breakfast

2. During my commute

3. In conversation with someone

4. In my five-to-nine after my nine-to-five

5. An unexpected moment

Today's glimmers:

1. My coffee was perfect—strong and steaming hot—and the smell woke me up and energized me for the day. I drank my first sip with my eyes closed and felt a moment of complete peace.

2. Even though I got out the door late this morning, I caught every single green light on the way to work. I ended up being perfectly on time, and it was deeply satisfying.

3. I had an amazing conversation with my boss today after a long stint of imposter syndrome. She reassured me that I'm doing a great job, and that if I keep it up, good things are en route. After a rough few weeks feeling like I'm spread too thin, it was just the morale boost I needed to continue feeling professionally inspired.

4. Today was my first post-work walk in the springtime, when the sun is still high in the sky upon my return home. It felt nice to get some sunshine after so much screen time. I listened to my favorite podcast and got some much-needed exercise to stretch my legs, which really helped alleviate some accumulating anxiety.

5. I completely forgot that I had bought myself mint chocolate chip ice cream during my grocery shopping over the weekend. I was feeling like I needed a sweet treat with my pre-bedtime tea and was devastated that I had nothing to satisfy it . . . until I opened the freezer and was smacked with childlike feelings of joy and eagerness. I grabbed a spoon, ate it straight from the pint, and went to bed feeling satiated.

Now that you know the drill, go forth and glimmer!

daily glimmer intention:

1 _____

2 _____

3 _____

4 _____

5 _____

today's glimmers:

1

2

3

4

5

daily glimmer intention:

1

2

3

4

5

today's glimmers:

1

2

3

4

5

daily glimmer intention:

1 _____

2 _____

3 _____

4 _____

5 _____

today's glimmers:

1

2

3

4

5

daily glimmer intention:

1

2

3

4

5

today's glimmers:

1

2

3

4

5

daily glimmer intention:

1 _____

2 _____

3 _____

4 _____

5 _____

today's glimmers:

1

2

3

4

5

daily glimmer intention:

1

2

3

4

5

today's glimmers:

1

2

3

4

5

daily glimmer intention:

today's glimmers:

1

2

3

4

5

daily glimmer intention:

1 _____

2 _____

3 _____

4 _____

5 _____

today's glimmers:

1

2

3

4

5

daily glimmer intention:

 1

 2

 3

 4

 5

today's glimmers:

1

2

3

4

5

daily glimmer intention:

 1

 2

 3

 4

 5

today's glimmers:

1

2

3

4

5

daily glimmer intention:

1 _____

2 _____

3 _____

4 _____

5 _____

today's glimmers:

1

2

3

4

5

daily glimmer intention:

1 _____

2 _____

3 _____

4 _____

5 _____

today's glimmers:

1

2

3

4

5

daily glimmer intention:

1 _____

2 _____

3 _____

4 _____

5 _____

today's glimmers:

1

2

3

4

5

daily glimmer intention:

1 _____

2 _____

3 _____

4 _____

5 _____

today's glimmers:

1

2

3

4

5

daily glimmer intention:

today's glimmers:

1

_____

_____

_____

2

_____

_____

_____

3

_____

_____

_____

4

_____

_____

_____

5

_____

_____

_____

daily glimmer intention:

1 _____

2 _____

3 _____

4 _____

5 _____

today's glimmers:

1

2

3

4

5

daily glimmer intention:

1 _____

2 _____

3 _____

4 _____

5 _____

today's glimmers:

1

2

3

4

5

daily glimmer intention:

1

2

3

4

5

today's glimmers:

1

2

3

4

5

daily glimmer intention:

1 _____

2 _____

3 _____

4 _____

5 _____

today's glimmers:

1

2

3

4

5

daily glimmer intention:

1

2

3

4

5

today's glimmers:

1

2

3

4

5

daily glimmer intention:

today's glimmers:

1

2

3

4

5

daily glimmer intention:

1 _____

2 _____

3 _____

4 _____

5 _____

today's glimmers:

1

2

3

4

5

daily glimmer intention:

1 _____

2 _____

3 _____

4 _____

5 _____

today's glimmers:

1

2

3

4

5

daily glimmer intention:

1 _____

2 _____

3 _____

4 _____

5 _____

today's glimmers:

1

2

3

4

5

daily glimmer intention:

1 _____

2 _____

3 _____

4 _____

5 _____

today's glimmers:

1

2

3

4

5

daily glimmer intention:

today's glimmers:

1

2

3

4

5

daily glimmer intention:

1. _____

2. _____

3. _____

4. _____

5. _____

today's glimmers:

1

2

3

4

5

daily glimmer intention:

1. _____

2. _____

3. _____

4. _____

5. _____

today's glimmers:

1

2

3

4

5

daily glimmer intention:

1 _____

2 _____

3 _____

4 _____

5 _____

today's glimmers:

1

2

3

4

5

daily glimmer intention:

today's glimmers:

1

2

3

4

5

daily glimmer intention:

1 _____

2 _____

3 _____

4 _____

5 _____

today's glimmers:

1

2

3

4

5

daily glimmer intention:

1 _____

2 _____

3 _____

4 _____

5 _____

today's glimmers:

1

2

3

4

5

daily glimmer intention:

1

2

3

4

5

today's glimmers:

1

2

3

4

5

daily glimmer intention:

1. _____

2. _____

3. _____

4. _____

5. _____

today's glimmers:

1

2

3

4

5

daily glimmer intention:

1

2

3

4

5

today's glimmers:

1

2

3

4

5

daily glimmer intention:

today's glimmers:

1

2

3

4

5

daily glimmer intention:

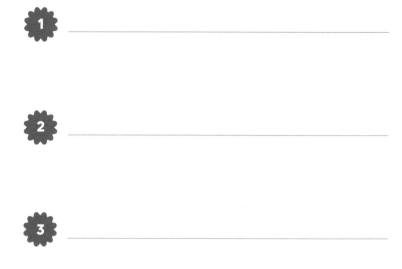

1 _____

2 _____

3 _____

4 _____

5 _____

today's glimmers:

1

2

3

4

5

daily glimmer intention:

1 _____

2 _____

3 _____

4 _____

5 _____

today's glimmers:

1

2

3

4

5

daily glimmer intention:

1 _____

2 _____

3 _____

4 _____

5 _____

today's glimmers:

1

2

3

4

5

daily glimmer intention:

1

2

3

4

5

today's glimmers:

1

2

3

4

5

daily glimmer intention:

1

2

3

4

5

today's glimmers:

1

2

3

4

5

daily glimmer intention:

1

2

3

4

5

today's glimmers:

1

2

3

4

5

daily glimmer intention:

1

2

3

4

5

today's glimmers:

1

2

3

4

5

daily glimmer intention:

1.

2.

3.

4.

5.

today's glimmers:

1

2

3

4

5

daily glimmer intention:

1 _____

2 _____

3 _____

4 _____

5 _____

today's glimmers:

1

2

3

4

5

daily glimmer intention:

1  _____

2  _____

3  _____

4 _____

5 _____

today's glimmers:

1

2

3

4

5

daily glimmer intention:

1

2

3

4

5

today's glimmers:

1

2

3

4

5

daily glimmer intention:

1 _____

2 _____

3 _____

4 _____

5 _____

today's glimmers:

1

2

3

4

5

---

daily glimmer intention:

1 _____

2 _____

3 _____

4 _____

5 _____

today's glimmers:

1

2

3

4

5

daily glimmer intention:

1 _____

2 _____

3 _____

4 _____

5 _____

today's glimmers:

1

2

3

4

5

daily glimmer intention:

1

2

3

4

5

today's glimmers:

1

2

3

4

5

daily glimmer intention:

1 _____

2 _____

3 _____

4 _____

5 _____

today's glimmers:

1

2

3

4

5

daily glimmer intention:

1 _____

2 _____

3 _____

4 _____

5 _____

today's glimmers:

1

2

3

4

5

daily glimmer intention:

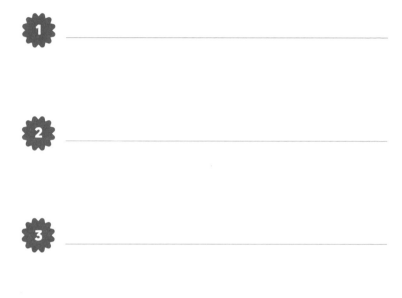

1 _____

2 _____

3 _____

4 _____

5 _____

today's glimmers:

1

2

3

4

5

daily glimmer intention:

1  _____

2 _____

3 _____

4 _____

5 _____

today's glimmers:

1

2

3

4

5

daily glimmer intention:

1.

2.

3.

4.

5.

today's glimmers:

1

2

3

4

5

daily glimmer intention:

1 _____

2 _____

3 _____

4 _____

5 _____

today's glimmers:

1

2

3

4

5

daily glimmer intention:

1. _____

2. _____

3. _____

4. _____

5. _____

today's glimmers:

1

2

3

4

5

daily glimmer intention:

1 _____

2 _____

3 _____

4 _____

5 _____

today's glimmers:

1

2

3

4

5

daily glimmer intention:

1

2

3

4

5

today's glimmers:

1

2

3

4

5

daily glimmer intention:

1

2

3

4

5

today's glimmers:

1

2

3

4

5

daily glimmer intention:

1 _____

2 _____

3 _____

4 _____

5 _____

today's glimmers:

1

2

3

4

5

daily glimmer intention:

1

2

3

4

5

today's glimmers:

1

2

3

4

5

daily glimmer intention:

1 _____

2 _____

3 _____

4 _____

5 _____

today's glimmers:

1

2

3

4

5

daily glimmer intention:

1 _____

2 _____

3 _____

4 _____

5 _____

today's glimmers:

1

2

3

4

5